D0419022
WITHDRAWN FOR SALE

THE BIG BOOK OF TRUMP

Published by Blink Publishing
2.25, The Plaza, 535 Kings Road, Chelsea Harbour, London, SW10 0SZ

www.blinkpublishing.co.uk

facebook.com/blinkpublishing
twitter.com/blinkpublishing

Hardback – 978-1-78870-053-5
Ebook – 978-1-78870-054-2

A CIP catalogue of this book is available from the British Library.

Design by Clarkevanmeurs Design Ltd

Printed and bound in Italy

1 3 5 7 9 10 8 6 4 2

Blink Publishing is an imprint of Bonnier Books UK
www.bonnierbooks.co.uk

To Vladimir, with love.

CONTENTS

Introduction 6

★ The Donald Tax Return 8
★ The Donald Waste Paper Game 9
★ Things that The Donald is Best at (Part 1) 10
★ Trump Nuclear Button 11
★ Humble Pie Recipe 12
★ Match the Comment to the Country or 'Country' 14
★ Employee Shooting Gallery 16
★ Draw The Donald on Mount Rushmore 18
★ Humpty Trumpy Dot-to-Dot 20
★ Trump Cheeseburger Maze 22
★ The Donald's Health Questionnaire 24
★ The Donald's Inauguration Speech Word Cloud 25
★ The Donald's Film and TV Cameos 26
★ 6 Things The Donald is a Big Fan of 27
★ Design Your Own Trump Mini-golf Hole 28
★ The Donald in Quotes… Climate Change 30
★ Secret Service Codenames 32
★ Royal Flush 34
★ Who Said It? 36
★ The Trump Riddle 38
★ Dinner with The Donald 39
★ Measure Your Hand Against The Donald's 40
★ Give Her a Ring 41
★ The Donald in Quotes… Women 42

★ Species Named After Trump 43
★ Glue the Toupée on the Trump 44
★ Match the Insult to the Person 46
★ Things The Donald is Best at (Part 2) 47
★ Donald J. Trump Presidential Library 48
★ Trumpopoly 50
★ Covfefe Granita 52
★ A Hard Act to Follow 54
★ The Donald in Quotes... Russia 55
★ Snakes & Elevators 56
★ Donald's Alternative Business Successes 58
★ It's Mueller Time! 59
★ Colour in The Donald's Boxers 60
★ Four-Legged Friend Finder 62
★ President Pence 64
★ Gone Golfing 66
★ The Happy Couple 68
★ Count the Crowd 70
★ Political Party Flip Flop 72
★ Emoji Catchphrases 74
★ The Donald in Quotes... Celebrity Feuds 75
★ The Donald Guide to Handshakes 76
★ What Shade is the Donald Today? 78
★ The Donald in Quotes... Race Relations 79
★ Press Room Seating Chart 80
★ Packing The Donald's Suitcase 82
★ The Donald in Quotes... Immigration 83
★ We Shall Overcomb 84
★ War of the Words 86
★ Trump Dictionary 88
★ The Great Inventor 89
★ A Day in the Life of The Donald 90
★ The Donald in Quotes... LGBTQ 91
★ Colour in the Seal 92

Answers 94
Picture Credits 96

INTRODUCTION

Welcome to *The Big Book of Trump*. This really is a **tremendous**, **beautiful** book, it really is. We've got some great things in here: Trump mini golf; Trump riddles; the Donald J. Trump presidential library. We've even included a fabulous recipe for Covfefe Granita – which is absolutely delicious, by the way. **Beautiful! It's so beautiful!**

So ignore the Fake News, the crooked media and the failing *New York Times*: ***The Big Book of Trump*** is a celebration of all things The Donald – a **tremendous**, **amazing** and **STRONG** book that's probably the **greatest** tome ever published. It's **unbelievable!**

Completely unbelievable!

You guys are gonna **love** this! Have a **great** time!

The Editor

THE DONALD

Form **1040** Department of the Treasury – Internal Tax Service (99)

Individual Income Tax Return | **2018**

First Name and Initial: Donald, The Last Name: Trump

Home Address: The White House

City: Washington D.C.

Country name: The (soon to be great again) United States of America

Income:

Donators	Amount
Vladivar Puttanesca	1 election
Luke Luckscan	1 white hat and cloak
Lucy Ferr	1 soul
Sharri Tee	Not a dime since 2005

For disclosure, privacy and paperwork reduction, see previous administration.

Form **1040**

THE DONALD WASTE PAPER GAME

(screw up the following into a ball and chuck away!)

THINGS THAT THE DONALD IS BEST AT (PART 1)

KNOWING THE BIBLE

'Nobody reads the Bible more than me.'

FEBRUARY 2016

RESPECTING WOMEN

'Nobody has more respect for women than Donald Trump!'

MARCH 2016

WALLS

'Nobody builds walls better than me.'

OCTOBER 2016

RENEWABLES

'I know more about renewables than any human being on Earth.'

APRIL 2016

BANKING

'Nobody knows banking better than I do'

FEBRUARY 2016

MONEY

'I understand money better than anybody.'

JUNE 2016

TAXES

'I think nobody knows more about taxes than I do, maybe in the history of the world. Nobody knows more about taxes.'

MAY 2016

DEBT

'Nobody knows more about debt. I'm like the king. I love debt.'

MAY 2016

TRUMP

NUCLEAR BUTTON

HUMBLE PIE RECIPE

Ingredients

500 g/2 cups shortcrust pastry
8 Orange Pippin apples (I prefer apples that remind me of my complexion)
3 tablespoons flour
6 teaspoons ground cinnamon
300 g/1 cup white (the best type) sugar, plus extra for dredging

Equipment

20-cm gold-plated pie dish

This pie is the greatest pie. And it is much more humble than you would understand.

Preheat the oven to 200°C (400°F). Ask an adult to help if your tiny hands can't turn the knob.

Get woman to roll out the pastry into two equal portions wide enough so one half can line the bottom of the pie dish.

Peel, core and thickly slice the apples, and cover with the flour, sugar and cinnamon. Alternatively, make America grate again by using a cheese grater. Pile into the pie dish.

Use the remaining pastry to top the pie.

Brush with water and dredge lightly with remaining sugar. Bake for 20–25 minutes until pastry is golden brown.

Do not put penis in pie.

TRUMP PIE
'NO ONE MAKES A BETTER PIE THAN ME'

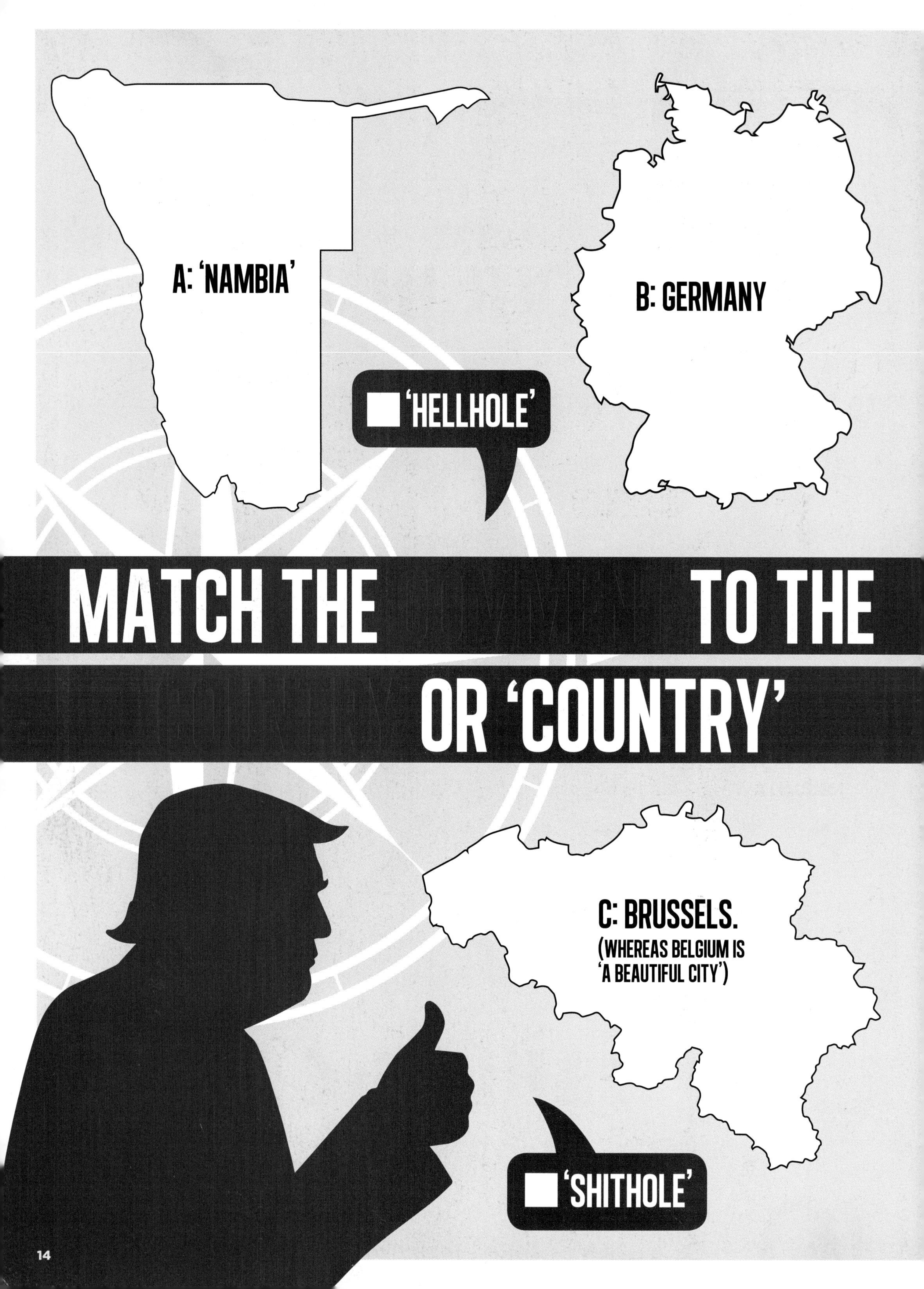
MATCH THE COMMENT TO THE
COUNTRY OR 'COUNTRY'
A: 'NAMBIA'
B: GERMANY
'HELLHOLE'
C: BRUSSELS.
(WHEREAS BELGIUM IS
'A BEAUTIFUL CITY')
'SHITHOLE'

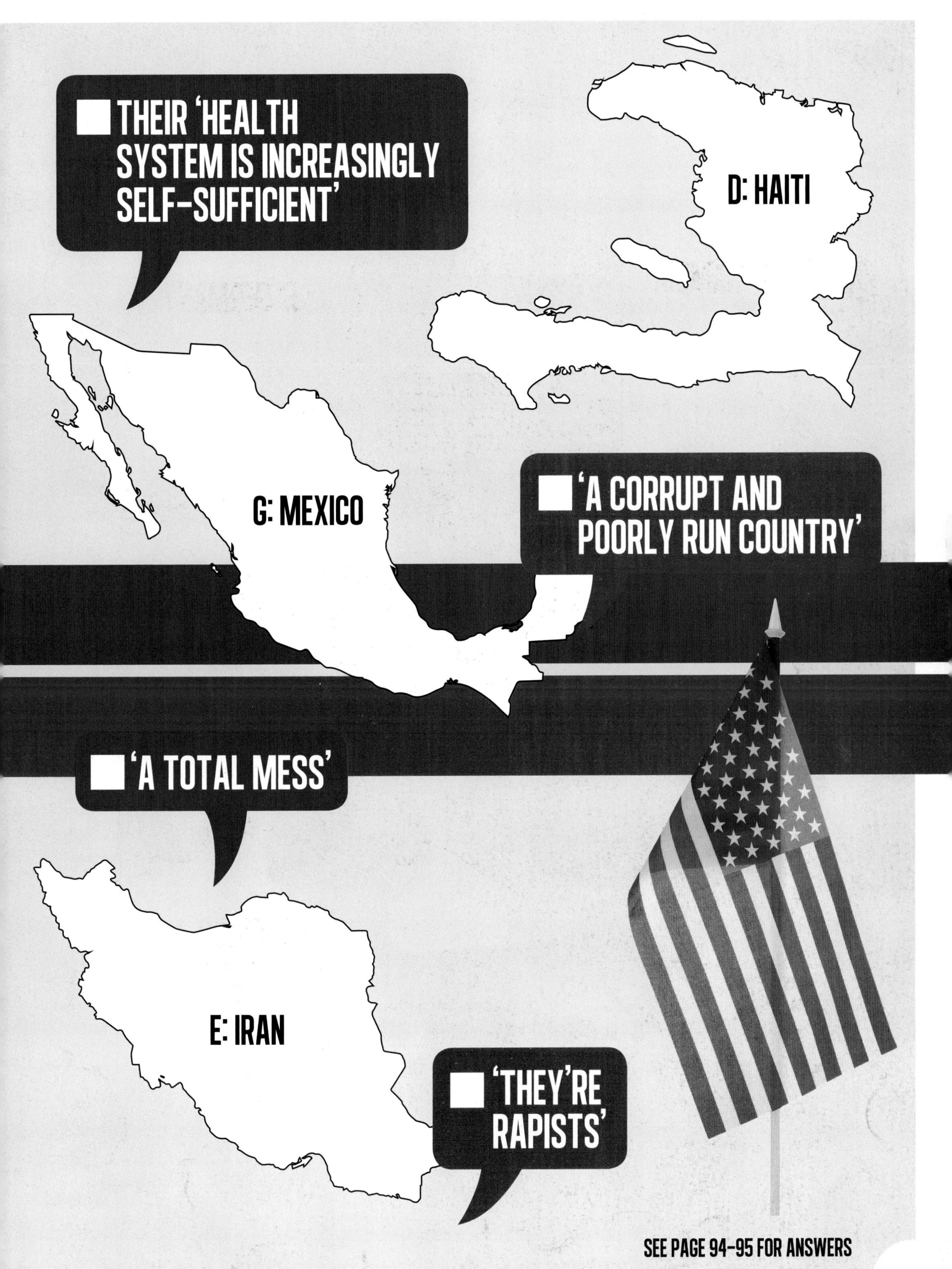

SEE PAGE 94–95 FOR ANSWERS

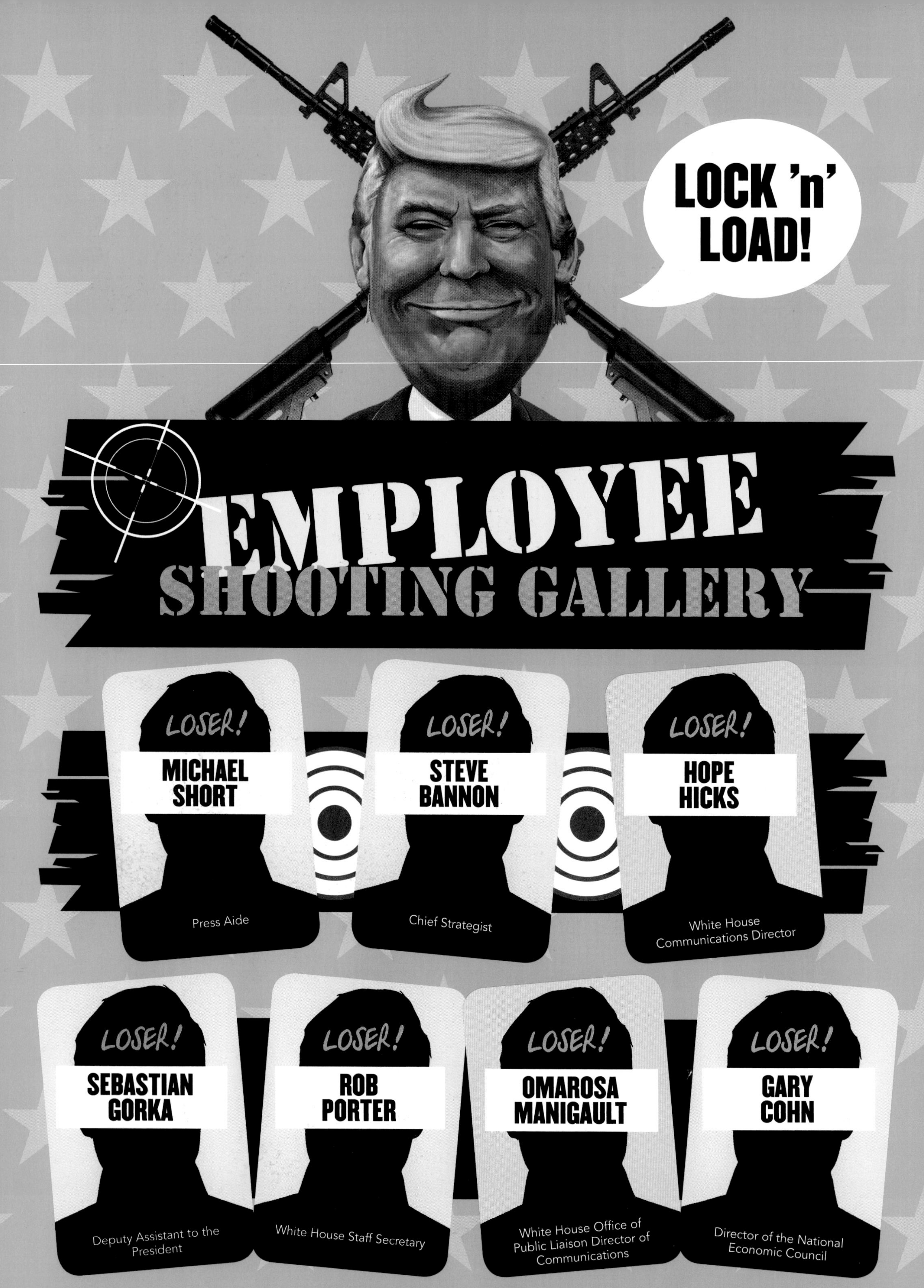
LOCK 'n' LOAD!
EMPLOYEE SHOOTING GALLERY
LOSER!
MICHAEL SHORT
Press Aide
LOSER!
STEVE BANNON
Chief Strategist
LOSER!
HOPE HICKS
White House Communications Director
LOSER!
SEBASTIAN GORKA
Deputy Assistant to the President
LOSER!
ROB PORTER
White House Staff Secretary
LOSER!
OMAROSA MANIGAULT
White House Office of Public Liaison Director of Communications
LOSER!
GARY COHN
Director of the National Economic Council

LOSER!
MICHAEL FLYNN
National Security Adviser
FIRED!
PREET BHARARA
US attorney for the Southern District of New York
LOSER!
BRENDA FITZGERALD
Center for Disease Control and Prevention Director
FIRED!
REX TILLERSON
Secretary of State
FIRED!
ANDREW MCCABE
FBI Deputy Director
LOSER!
KATIE WALSH
Deputy White House Chief of Staff
FIRED!
JAMES COMEY
FBI Director
LOSER!
REINCE PRIEBUS
Chief of Staff
LOSER!
MICHAEL DUBKE
Communications Director
FIRED!
SALLY YATES
US Deputy Attorney General
LOSER!
ANTHONY SCARAMUCCI
Communications Director
LOSER!
SEAN SPICER
Press Secretary
LOSER!
H.R. MCMASTER
National Security Adviser
LOSER!
TOM BOSSERT
National Security Adviser

The Donald has done more than enough to earn his rightful place next to the our legendary Presidents carved on Mount Rushmore in South Dakota. Please add your own drawing of the Donald in the space provided.

Humpty Trumpy

Join the dots to uncover The Donald's finishing touches to his Wall design.

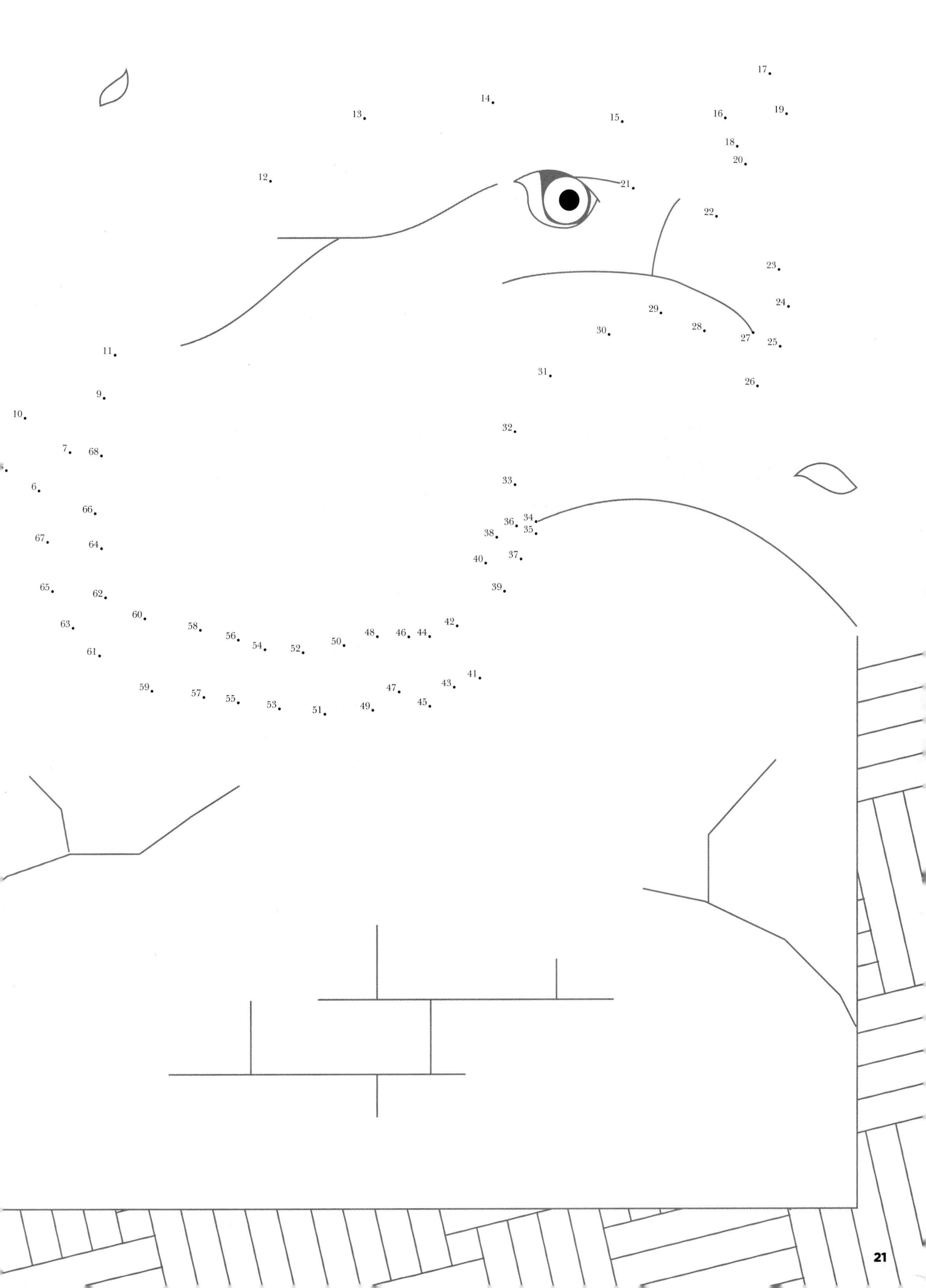

Can Trump find his way to the cheeseburger?

There's a cheeseburger waiting for The Donald on his desk in the Oval Office. Can you guide him to it? However, there are a number of obstacles to overcomb (sorry, I mean overcome).

F.B.I.
MIGUEL

The Donald's health questionnaire

'If elected, Mr Trump, I can state unequivocally, will be the healthiest individual ever elected to the presidency.'

Harold Bornstein, The Donald's personal physician, December 2015

1. How would you describe your height?
2. How would you describe your weight?
3. How would you describe your intelligence?
4. How would you describe your emotional state?
5. How much exercise do you do each day?
6. How would you describe your overall health?

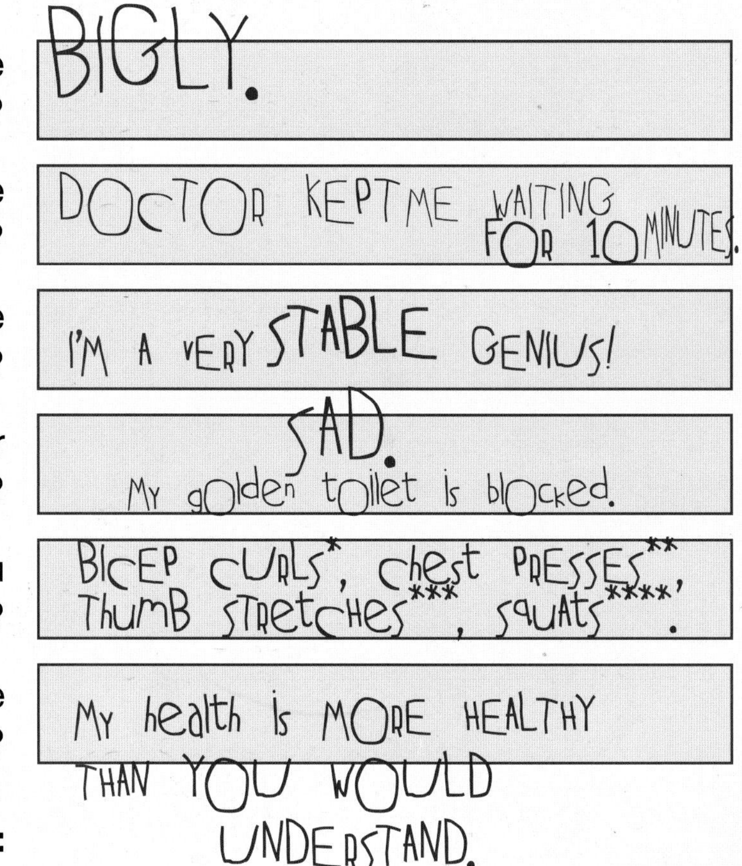

Notes:

* lifting cheeseburgers

** pushing paper off his desk

*** pressing buttons on his phone

**** to hide under his desk when Melania comes in

The Donald's
Inauguration
Speech Word Cloud
moment
many
became
celebrate
Now
even
like
celebrated
Bless
years
power
anyone
must
men
Great
good
way
across
nation
matters
20th
starting
get
everyone
people
left
dreams
gathered
success
weve
wealth
jobs
Earth
celebration
January
pain
strength
one
new
talk
life
old
back
American
controlled
action
world
Make
stops
struggling
remembered
seek
Thank
city
let
Country
oath
controls
little
rulers
nations
Safe
truly
every
another
changes
roads
day
right
bring
heart
industry
God
borders
face
long
capital
Together
never
America

The Donald has graced our screens with numerous memorable performances over the decades. In 2007, he was honoured with a star on Hollywood Boulevard thanks to the success of *The Apprentice*. In 1989, he was bestowed with a rather different honour, winning the Worst Supporting Actor category at the 11th Golden Raspberry Awards for his cameo in *Ghosts Can't Do It*.

Can you name the following TV shows and films that The Donald has appeared in from the cryptic clues?

See pages 94–95 for answers

★ Second solitary dwelling

★ 14 days left on the contract

★ There's only one Mr Big in this town

★ Wildlife park spacecraft

★ Twist town

★ New Heir of a Hollywood neighbourhood

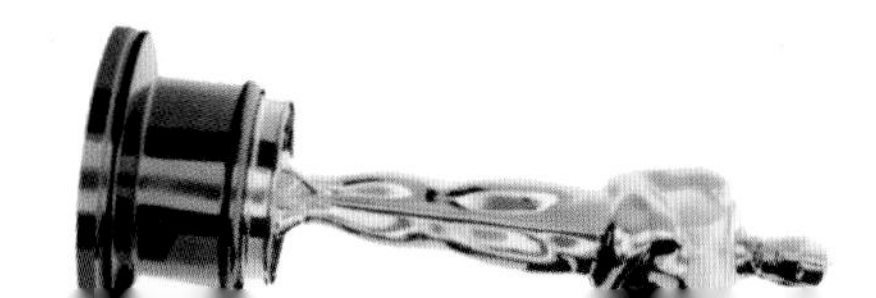

6 THINGS THE DONALD IS A BIG FAN OF.

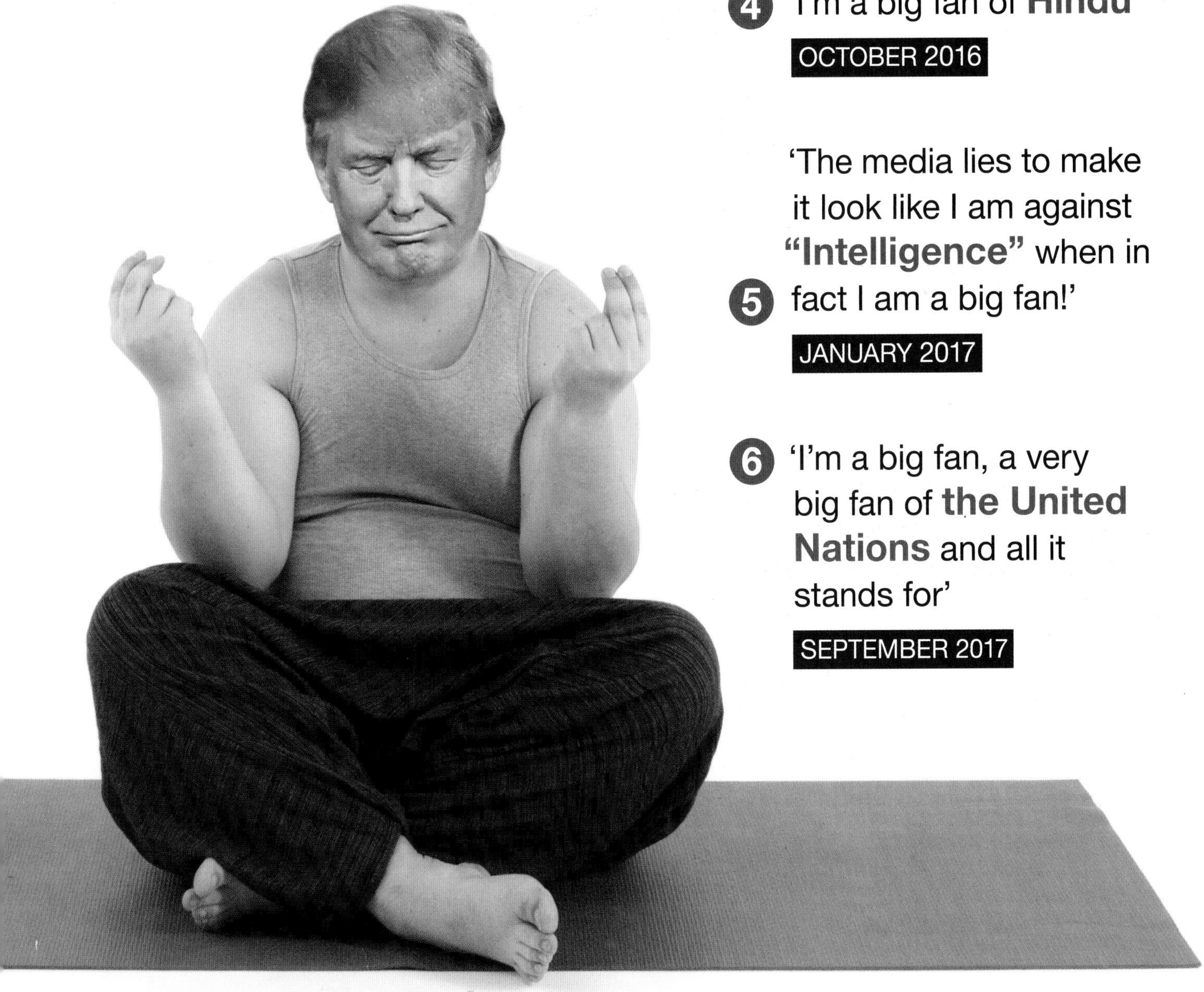

1. 'I'm a big fan of **Israel**'
   MAY 2013

2. 'I'm a big **history** fan'
   NOVEMBER 2015

3. 'I am a big fan of **the Kurds**'
   JULY 2016

4. 'I'm a big fan of **Hindu**'
   OCTOBER 2016

5. 'The media lies to make it look like I am against **"Intelligence"** when in fact I am a big fan!'
   JANUARY 2017

6. 'I'm a big fan, a very big fan of **the United Nations** and all it stands for'
   SEPTEMBER 2017

DESIGN YOUR OWN
TRUMP
MINI-GOLF
HOLE

You've been asked to design a mini-golf hole on the lawn of the White House!

CLIMATE CHANGE

'The concept of global warming was created by and for the Chinese in order to make U.S. manufacturing non-competitive.'
November 2012

'It's really cold outside, they are calling it a major freeze, weeks ahead of normal. Man, we could use a big fat dose of global warming!' October 2015

'In the East, it could be the COLDEST New Year's Eve on record. Perhaps we could use a little bit of that good old Global Warming that our Country, but not other countries, was going to pay TRILLIONS OF DOLLARS to protect against. Bundle up!'
December 2017

'There is a cooling, and there's a heating. I mean, look, it used to not be climate change, it used to be global warming. That wasn't working too well because it was getting too cold all over the place.' January 2018

'The ice caps were going to melt, they were going to be gone by now, but now they're setting records. They're at a record level.' January 2018

SECRET SERVICE CODENAMES

Match the codenames to the real names!

The US Secret Service uses codenames for presidents, members of the First Family and prominent figures in the administration, as well as for specialised vehicles, rooms and agencies. Some esteemed visitors are also given unique codenames.

RENEGADE

MOGUL

UNICORN

EVERGREEN

KITTYHAWK

SEARCHLIGHT

EAGLE

LACE

TIMBERWOLF

RAWHIDE

See pages 94–95 for answers

Royal FLUSH

The Donald has run out of gold-leaf toilet paper and copies of Barack Obama's birth certificate to wipe his behind on. Calamity! He's commissioned you to come up with a new design.

BARACK OBAMA
MY VISION FOR A BETTER AMERICA

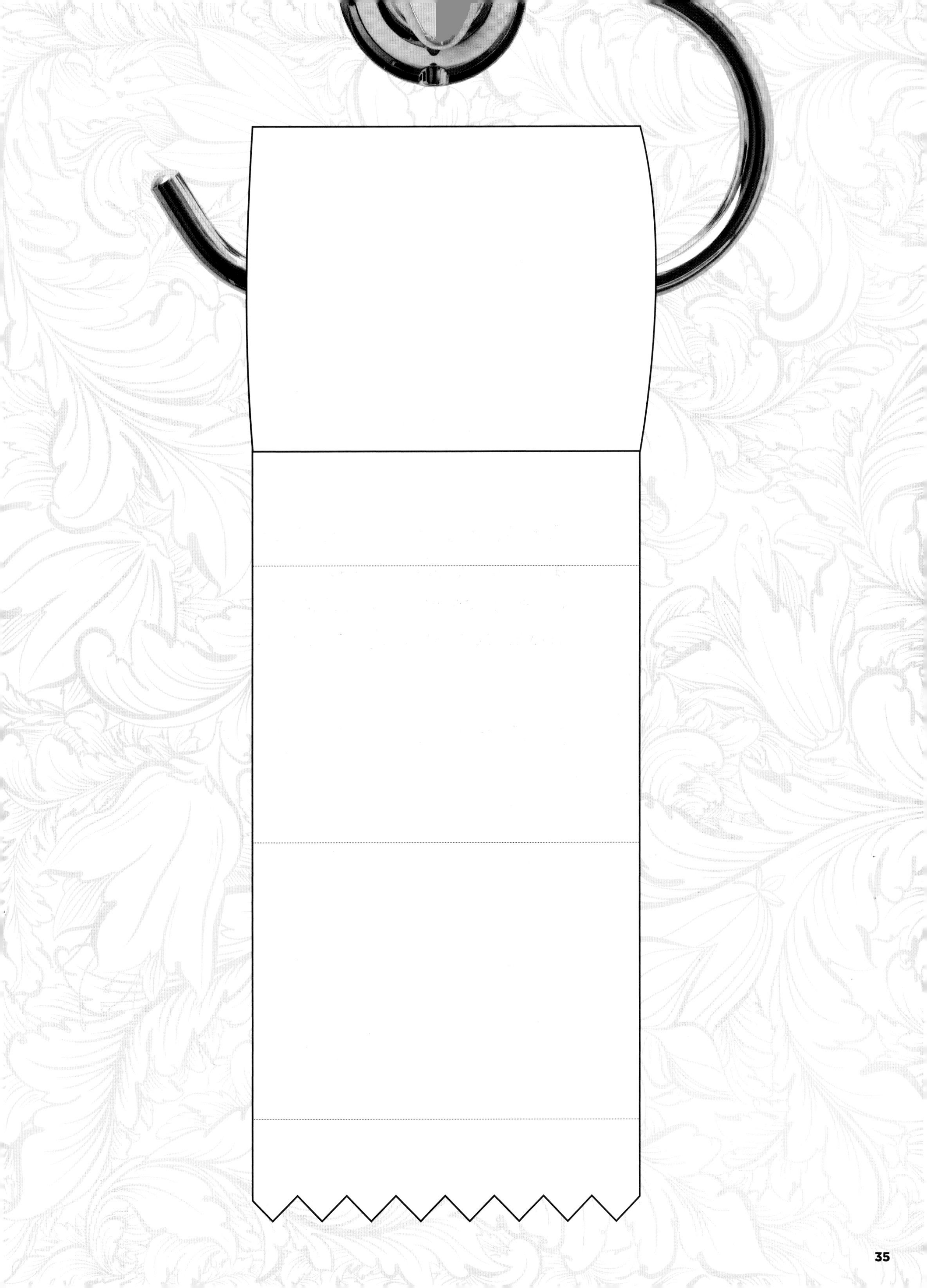

WHO SAID IT?

Find The Donald's words amid the soundbites of the not-so magnificent seven below:

'I'm not a dictator. It's just that I have a grumpy face.'

'If you win, you need not have to explain. If you lose, you should be there to explain!'

'I trust no one, not even myself.'

'Those who do not love me do not deserve to live.'

'The problem with me is that I am fifty or one hundred years ahead of my time.'

'I'm quite modest. I don't want to tell people I'm a leader.'

'I play to people's fantasies – I call it truthful hyperbole.'

see pages 94–95 for answers

ADOLF HITLER?

JOSEPH STALIN?

THE DONALD?

IDI AMIN?

RiDDLE

The Donald stands proudly at 6 feet 3 inches according to his doctor Ronny Jackson, yet when he stands side by side with the 6-foot-1-inch tall Barack Obama, The Donald looks marginally shorter. Can you account for the discrepancy?

See pages 94–95 for answer

DINNER WITH
THE DONALD
?

DINNER WITH
THE DONALD
Melania

R.S.V.P.
Sorry big D, I'm having a root canal

DINNER WITH
THE DONALD
Rupert M.

R.S.V.P.
What a f*****g idiot

DINNER WITH THE DONALD

The Donald is hosting a dinner party at the White House and can pick three people, living or dead. Sadly, two have already declined his offer. Can you pick three for him?

MEASURE YOUR HAND AGAINST THE DONALD'S

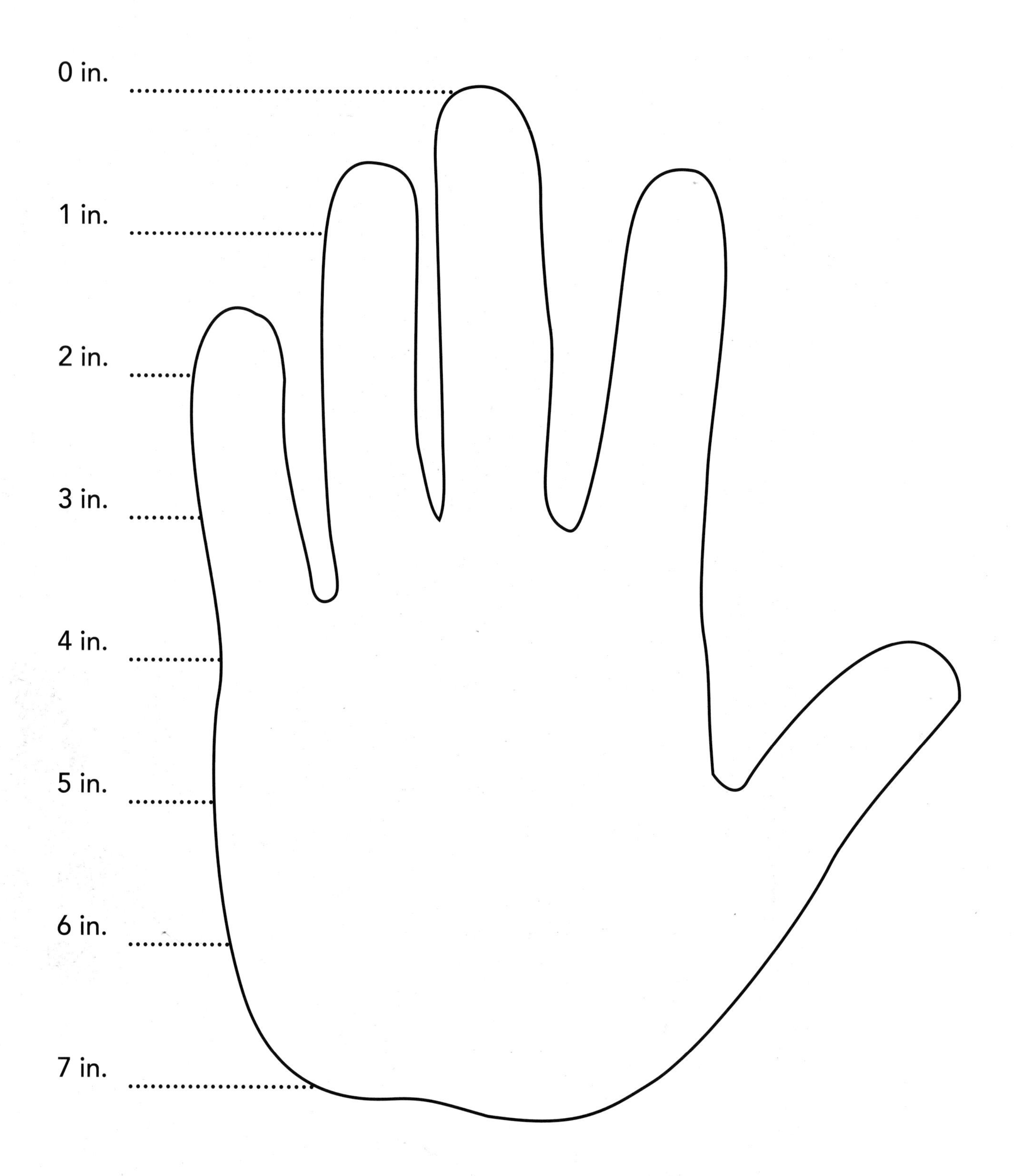

TRUMP

GIVE HER A RING

These are the most expensive engagement rings of all time. Melania is only number 5, but seeing as 5 is more than 1, it stands to reason that hers cost the most. And it's certainly the bigliest.

1

Elizabeth Taylor ($8.8 million ring made from a 33-carat Asscher cut Krupp Diamond bought at auction and given to her by Richard Burton)

2

Beyoncé Knowles ($5 million 18-carat flawless diamond by Lorraine Schwartz, given to her by Jay-Z)

3

Anna Kournikova (between $2.5 and $6 million 11-carat natural pink pear shape diamond, given to her by Enrique Iglesias)

4

Paris Hilton ($4.7 million 24-carat canary diamond ring, given to her by then-fiancé Paris Latsis)

5

Melania Trump ($3 million 12-carat ring given to her by the man, the myth, the legend).

WOMEN

'Women have one of the great acts of all time. The smart ones are very feminine and needy, but inside they are real killers.' *The Art of the Comeback*, 1997

'All of the women on *The Apprentice* flirted with me – consciously or unconsciously. That's to be expected.' *How To Get Rich*, 2004

'I'm automatically attracted to beautiful women – I just start kissing them. It's like a magnet. Just kiss. I don't even wait. When you're a star, they let you do it. You can do anything. Grab 'em by the pussy. You can do anything.' Secret recording of Donald talking to former *Access Hollywood* host Billy Bush, 2005

'I don't think Ivanka would do that although she does have a very nice figure. I've said if Ivanka weren't my daughter perhaps I'd be dating her.' March 2006

'Look at that face! Would anyone vote for that? Can you imagine that, the face of our next president?! I mean, she's a woman, and I'm not supposed to say bad things, but really, folks, come on. Are we serious?' (about Carly Fiorina, a rival presidential candidate) September 2015

'If Hillary Clinton can't satisfy her husband what makes her think she can satisfy America.' April 2015

'You could see there was blood coming out of her eyes. Blood coming out of her wherever.' (about Fox News anchor Megyn Kelly) August 2015

Species named after Trump

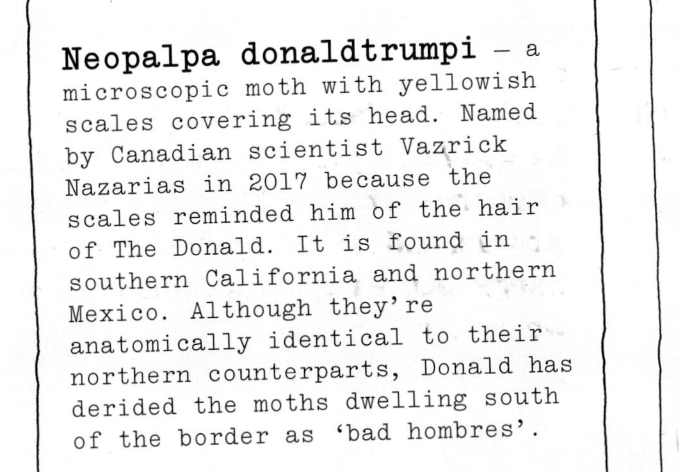

Neopalpa donaldtrumpi – a microscopic moth with yellowish scales covering its head. Named by Canadian scientist Vazrick Nazarias in 2017 because the scales reminded him of the hair of The Donald. It is found in southern California and northern Mexico. Although they're anatomically identical to their northern counterparts, Donald has derided the moths dwelling south of the border as 'bad hombres'.

Tetragramma donaldtrumpi – a species of fossil sea urchin discovered by William R. Thompson in 2016. A remnant of a bygone era, this prickly creature could plunge to extreme depths and measured only 1 inch long where it counts. Quite similar to the sea urchin then.

fibrous straw-like consistency

unnatural orange colouring

The Trump Caterpillar

The caterpillar of the Megalopyge opercularis moth, also known as the asp moth, bears a striking resemblance to The Donald's hair, leading to its colloquial name the 'Trump caterpillar'. Curiously, it is one of the most venomous insects in North America…

GLUE THE TOUPÉE ON THE TRUMP!

It's the game you've all been waiting for!

First cut out the toupée below. Stick the picture of The Donald up somewhere with some sticky tape. Dab the back of the toupée with glue, grab yourself a makeshift blindfold and try to glue the toupée on the Trump!

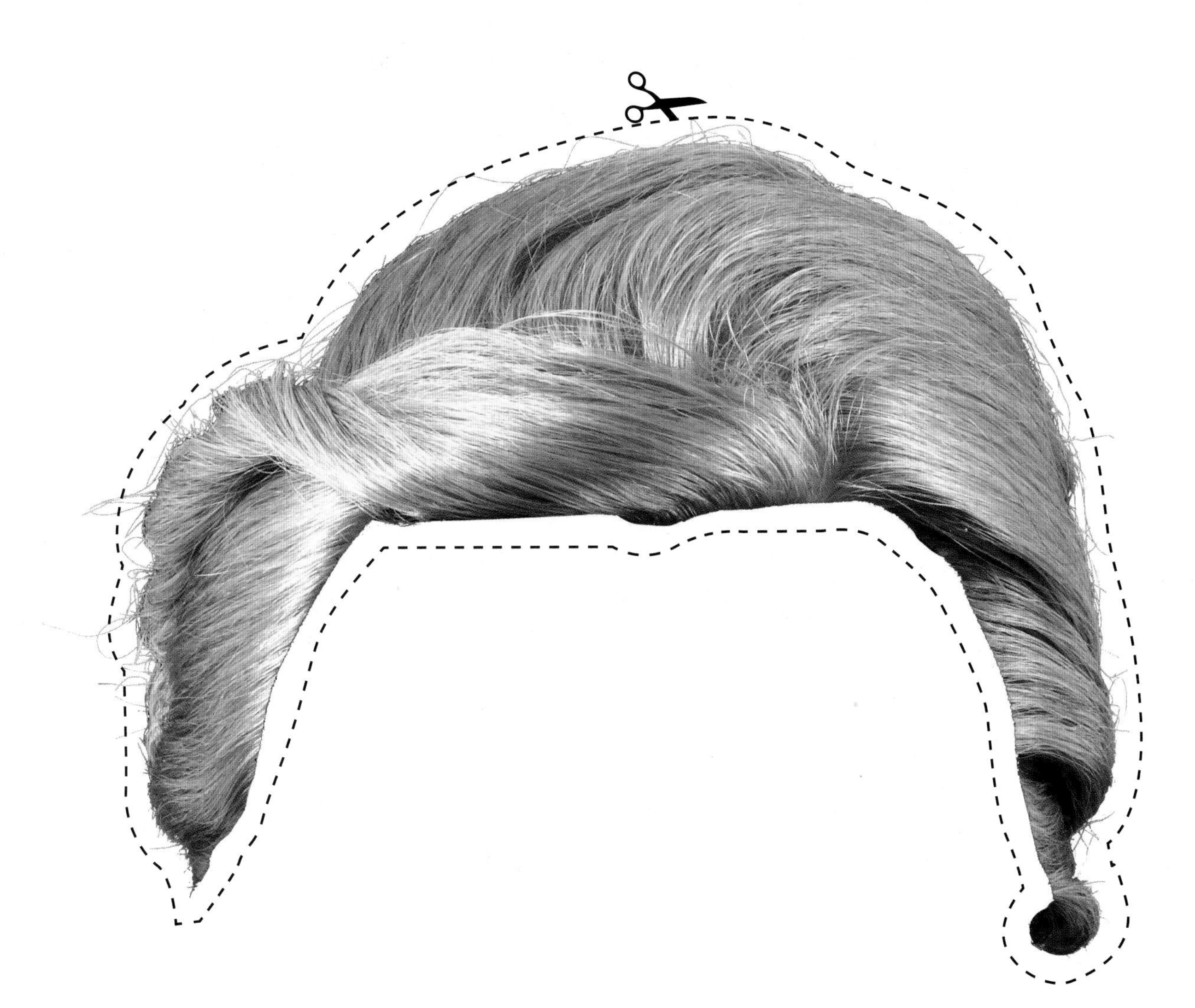

MATCH THE INSULT TO THE PERSON

'Always looking to start World War III.'

'Hillary flunky who lost big.'

'He just wants to sit down and go home to bed!'

'Had to bring in Mommy to take a slap at me.'

Bill Clinton

Whoopi Goldberg

Mitt Romney

Bernie Sanders

Jeb Bush

'There's never been anyone more abusive to women in politics.'

'Now in total freefall.'

'So awkward and goofy.'

'Mathematically dead and totally desperate.'

Meryl Streep

Ted Cruz

John McCain

see pages 94–95 for answers

THINGS THAT THE DONALD IS BEST AT (PART 2)

THE US SYSTEM OF GOVERNMENT

'Nobody knows the system better than I do.'

APRIL 2016

POLITICIANS

'Nobody knows politicians better than Donald Trump.'

FEBRUARY 2016

INFRASTRUCTURE

'Nobody in the history of this country has ever known so much about infrastructure as Donald Trump.'

JULY 2016

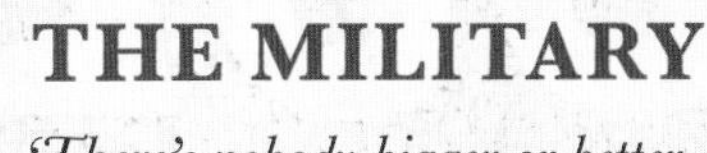

THE MILITARY

'There's nobody bigger or better at the military than I am.'

JUNE 2015

TRADE

'Nobody knows more about trade than me.'

MARCH 2016

ISIS

'I know more about ISIS [the Islamic State militant group] than the generals do. Believe me.'

NOVEMBER 2015

THE HORROR OF NUCLEAR

"There is nobody who understands the horror of nuclear more than me."

JUNE 2016

Donald J. Trump Presidential Library

Please include your suggestions for the Trump Presidential Library. The Donald's already left a few of his faves to start the collection.

HOME
MR NOISY
FIRE AND FURY
HUSTLER
PLAYBOY
SPOT THE DOG

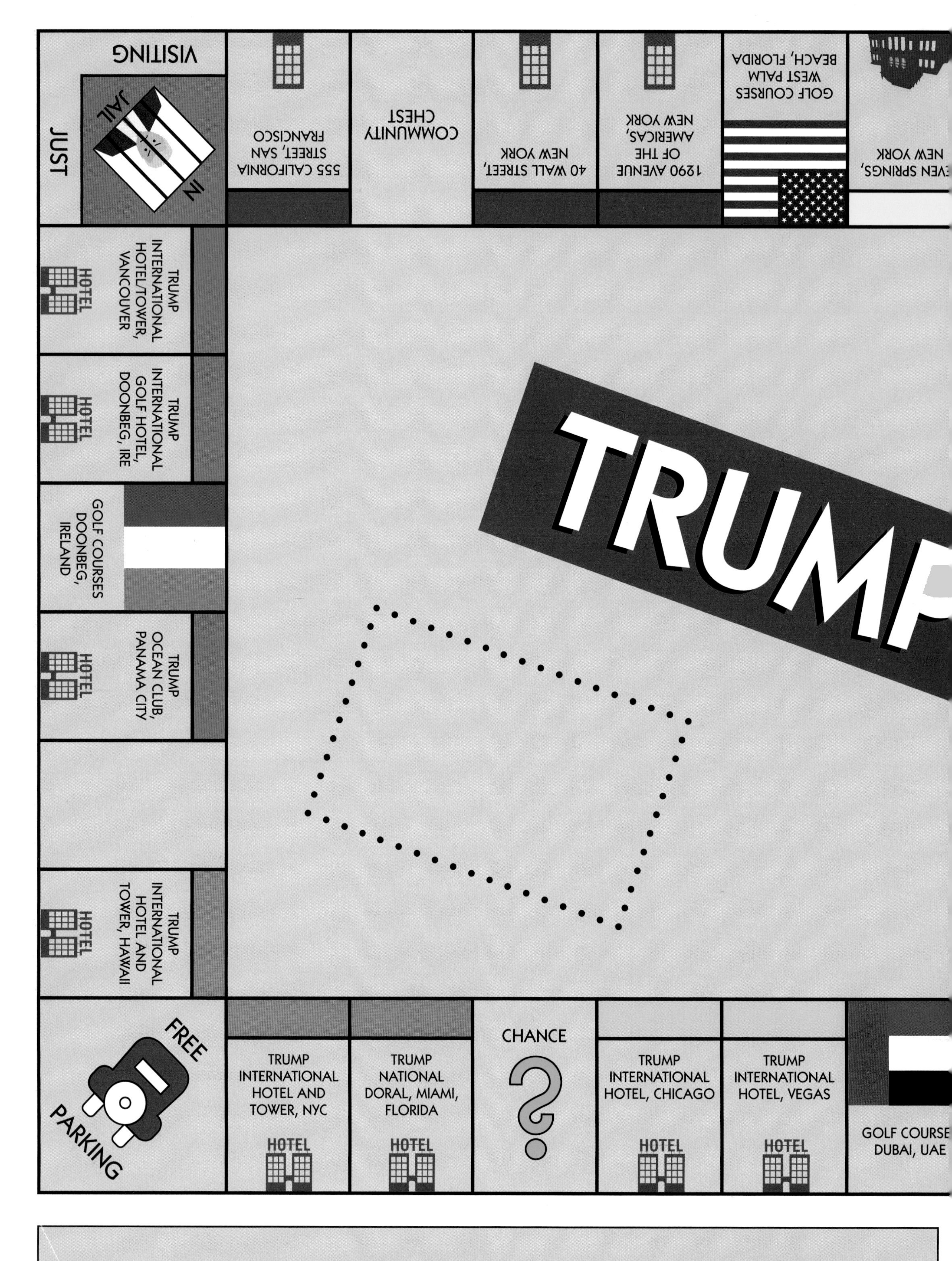
JUST
IN
JAIL
VISITING
555 CALIFORNIA STREET, SAN FRANCISCO
COMMUNITY CHEST
40 WALL STREET, NEW YORK
1290 AVENUE OF THE AMERICAS, NEW YORK
GOLF COURSES WEST PALM BEACH, FLORIDA
EVEN SPRINGS, NEW YORK
TRUMP INTERNATIONAL HOTEL/TOWER, VANCOUVER
HOTEL
TRUMP INTERNATIONAL GOLF HOTEL, DOONBEG, IRE
HOTEL
GOLF COURSES DOONBEG, IRELAND
TRUMP OCEAN CLUB, PANAMA CITY
HOTEL
TRUMP INTERNATIONAL HOTEL AND TOWER, HAWAII
HOTEL
TRUMP
FREE PARKING
TRUMP INTERNATIONAL HOTEL AND TOWER, NYC
HOTEL
TRUMP NATIONAL DORAL, MIAMI, FLORIDA
HOTEL
CHANCE
TRUMP INTERNATIONAL HOTEL, CHICAGO
HOTEL
TRUMP INTERNATIONAL HOTEL, VEGAS
HOTEL
GOLF COURSE DUBAI, UAE

806 NORTH RODEO DRIVE, LOS ANGELES
CHANCE
TRUMP
TRUMP VINEYARD, VIRGINIA
TRUMP PARC, NEW YORK
TRUMP PARK AVENUE, NEW YORK
GO
MAR-A-LAGO, FLORIDA
SUPER TAX
GOLF COURSES DOONBEG, IRELAND
TRUMP TOWER, FIFTH AVENUE, NEW YORK
CHANCE
THE WHITE HOUSE
OPOLY
TRUMP INTERNATIONAL HOTEL, WASHINGTON D.C.
HOTEL
INCOME TAX
WOLLMAN ICE RINK, CENTRAL PARK
TRUMP
CENTRAL PARK CAROUSEL, NYC
Trump
GO TO JAIL

COVFEFE GRANITA

Ingredients

600 ml/1 pint strong espresso coffee, hot
120 g/1 generous cup caster sugar, preferably golden like my glorious barnet
300 ml/10 fl oz double cream
1 vanilla pod/bean, seeds scraped out, or few drops vanilla essence
1 tablespoon icing sugar

With the surprising pale yellow topping, this dessert may remind you of someone...

Place a shallow baking dish in the freezer until it's colder than one of Melania's affectionate glances.

Stir and dissolve the caster sugar in the hot coffee and allow to cool.

Pour the cooled mixture into the baking dish and freeze for 45 minutes. If any liberal snowflakes (sorry, ice crystals) start to loiter around the outside, bring them forcibly into the liquid centre with a fork.

Check the dish again after another 20 minutes (this should give you enough time for a quick telephone call to Vladimir) and repeat the step above. Continue doing this until there are no liquid parts. Tip the granita into a Tupperware box until required.

Pre-chill a couple of glasses for your lady friends.

Add the cream, vanilla and sugar in a large bowl. Add some crushed ice (you shouldn't have a problem finding it – the ice caps are at record levels) and whip the mixture until it is a dropping consistency.

Serve the granita with the whipped cream toupée on top.

twit.com/realDonaldTrump

Presidenting for Dummies · moodyladies.com · howtowinfriendsandinfluencepeople · ToysRUs · SlapObama.com · JamesComeyfanclub

Tweets
Too many

Following
47

Followers
Debatable

Follow

A hard act to follow

@DonnieTrumpPrez

45th President of the United States of America (I know, right?)

Worlwide Trends

#DonaldTrumpTheMovie
#TrumpYourCat
#MakeDonaldDrumpfAgain
#PutinsPuppet
#MexicanRapists
#BatTrump
#Trumpocalypse
#LoveTrumpsHate
#ShitholePresident

The Donald only follows 47 people on Twitter. If we subtract his business ventures, members of his extended family, employees, former employees, *Apprentice* collaborators and several Fox News commentators, there are only three remaining. Can you guess them? Here are your clues:

Number 1: Former editor of the *News of the World*. Charming chap.

Number 2: Nine-time golf major winner from South Africa

Number 3: Famously had his head shaved by The Donald in a WWF wrestling ring in what was dubbed the 'Battle of the Billionaires'.

See pages 94–95 for answers

RUSSIA

'I own Miss Universe, I was in Russia, I was in Moscow recently and I spoke, indirectly and directly, with President Putin, who could not have been nicer, and we had a tremendous success.' May 2014

'I have no relationship with him other than he called me a genius. He said "Donald Trump is a genius and he is going to be the leader of the party and he's going to be the leader of the world or something".' February 2016

'Putin says very nice things about me. I think that's very nice and it has no effect on me other than I think it's very nice.' March 2016

'I think it was Russia,' (and Putin) 'should not be doing it.' (on hacking the Democratic National Committee in 2016)

'I think I could see myself meeting with Putin and meeting with Russia prior to the start of the administration... I think it would be wonderful.' October 2016

'Most politicians would have gone to a meeting like the one Don jr attended in order to get info on an opponent. That's politics!' (on his son's meeting with Russian lawyer Natalia Veselnitskaya to receive information from the Russians that would damage Hillary Clinton's Presidential campaign) July 2017

Snakes & Elevators
100
99
98
96
81
82
84
85
80
79
78
77
76
61
62
63
64
65
60
58
56
41
42
43
45
40
39
38
37
36
21
22
23
24
20
19
18
17
16
1
2
3
4
5

Snakes & Elevators

DONALD'S ALTERNATIVE BUSINESS SUCCESSES*

*** FAILURES**

BUSINESS

1 Donald J Trump Signature Collection (menswear fashion line)

2 GoTrump.com (travel website)

3 Trump Entertainment Resorts

4 *Trump* Magazine

5 Trump University

6 Trump Mortgage

7 Trump Network (marketing company)

8 Trump Steaks

9 Trump Shuttle (airline)

10 Trump Vodka

FATE

1 Launched in 2004 and discontinued in 2015 after comments Donald made about Mexicans

2 Launched in 2006 and closed in 2007

3 Founded in 1995 and filed for bankruptcy in 2004, 2009 and 2014

4 Founded in 2002 and ceased publication in 2009

5 Opened in 2005; effectively shut in 2010 after multiple lawsuits

6 Founded in 2005 and folded in 2007

7 Founded in 1997 and folded in 2012

8 Introduced in 2007 and discontinued the same year

9 Bought by The Donald in 1989 and sold at a knock-down price in 1992.

10 Launched in 2005 and ceased production in 2011; still popular in Israel though!

IT'S MUELLER TIME!

SUGGESTED INTERVIEW QUESTIONS FOR SPECIAL COUNSEL ROBERT MUELLER TO ASK THE DONALD:

1. ***PREY ON HIS WEAKNESSES:*** (Get attractive woman to enter the Oval Office door and ask): Mr President, Vladimir's on the phone for you. He's asking about his cheque. Shall I put him through?

2. ***FREAK HIM OUT:*** Mr President, I'm afraid I'm legally required to strap a shark fin to my back and play the *Jaws* theme tune throughout this interview.

3. ***TURN HIM ON:*** If you tell me the truth, I promise I'll roll up this copy of *Forbes* magazine and spank you until your posterior is Republican red.

4. ***BEFUDDLE HIM WITH DOUBLE NEGATIVES:*** So Mr President, it would be fair to say that you did not not collude with the Russians then? That's fair, isn't it not?

5. ***CONFUSE HIM WITH LANGUAGE HE DOESN'T UNDERSTAND:*** So, Mr President, just to stick to the basics, your propinquity with the Russian President did not lead to an excogitation to chicane the election thanks to an ad valorem disbursement? I must have a yes or no answer.

Colour in the Donald's boxers

The Donald likes to sleep commando, but he's finally allowed Melania to design him a special pair of boxers to sleep in. Can you provide the finishing touches and colour it in?

Four-legged friend finder

The Donald is the first President since Andrew Jackson (in office 1829–1837) not to have a four-legged friend at his side.

Benjamin Harrison (in office 1899–1893) had two opossums called Mr Reciprocity and Mr Protection; Teddy Roosevelt (in office 1901–1909) had a laughing hyena called Bill, offered as a gift by Emperor Menelik of Ethiopia, and Calvin Coolidge (in office 1923–1929) received 13 Pekin ducks as an Easter gift, which Mrs Coolidge tried to raise in a White House bathroom before admitting defeat and sending them to a zoo.

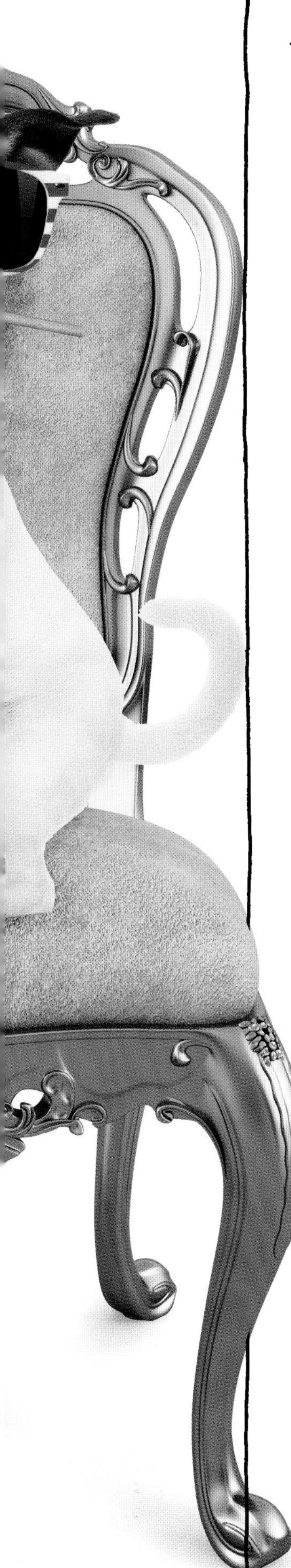

The Donald said it was 'low class' of Mike Pence to bring his dogs to Washington D.C., so it's up to you to change his mind and draw a suitable companion… oh, and come up with a suitable name too…

So Mueller Time sees the end of The Donald (SAD) and President Pence takes the mic. Here are some of Vice-President Pence's Greatest Hits:

PRESIDEN

'Don't ask that guy... he wants to hang them all!' (The Donald talking about Mike Pence's attitude towards the LGBT community)

'For years, we have gotten the message from the mouthpieces of the popular culture that you can have it all, career, kids and a two-car garage... Sure, you can have it all, but your day-care kids get the short end of the emotional stick.'

'Time for a quick reality check. Despite the hysteria from the political class and the media, *smoking doesn't kill.* In fact, two out of every three smokers does not die from a smoking-related illness.'

'Most climatologists agree that, at best, global warming is a theory about future climatic conditions and cannot be proven based upon the historic record.'

IT PENCE

'Frankly, condoms are a very, very poor protection against sexually transmitted diseases.'

'Global warming is a myth... There, I said it. Just like the "new Ice Age" scare of the 1970s, the environmental movement has found a new chant for their latest "Chicken Little" attempt to raise taxes and grow centralized governmental power. The chant is "the sky is warming! the sky is warming!" '

The Donald was a fierce critic of former Presidents playing golf while in office. The graphic below shows how many days the last four Presidents spent on the course during the first 100 days of their respective administrations.

'Can you believe that, with all of the problems and difficulties facing the U.S., President Obama spent the day playing golf. Worse than Carter.' The Donald, October 2014
'I'm going to be working for you, I'm not going to have time to go play golf.' The Donald, August 2016
1
19
GOLFUS MAXIMUS
Obama.
Trump.

The Happy Couple

The Donald is compiling a family photo album of happy memories with his beloved Melania by his side. He's having trouble choosing the right one, though…

(1) The 'glower'

(2) The 'I've hired a body double so I don't have to be near this creep'

(4) The 'I have to look at this man naked'
(4) 'Sadface'
(5) The 'where's the exit?'

Can you count the number of Trump supporters who have turned up to see The Donald speak?

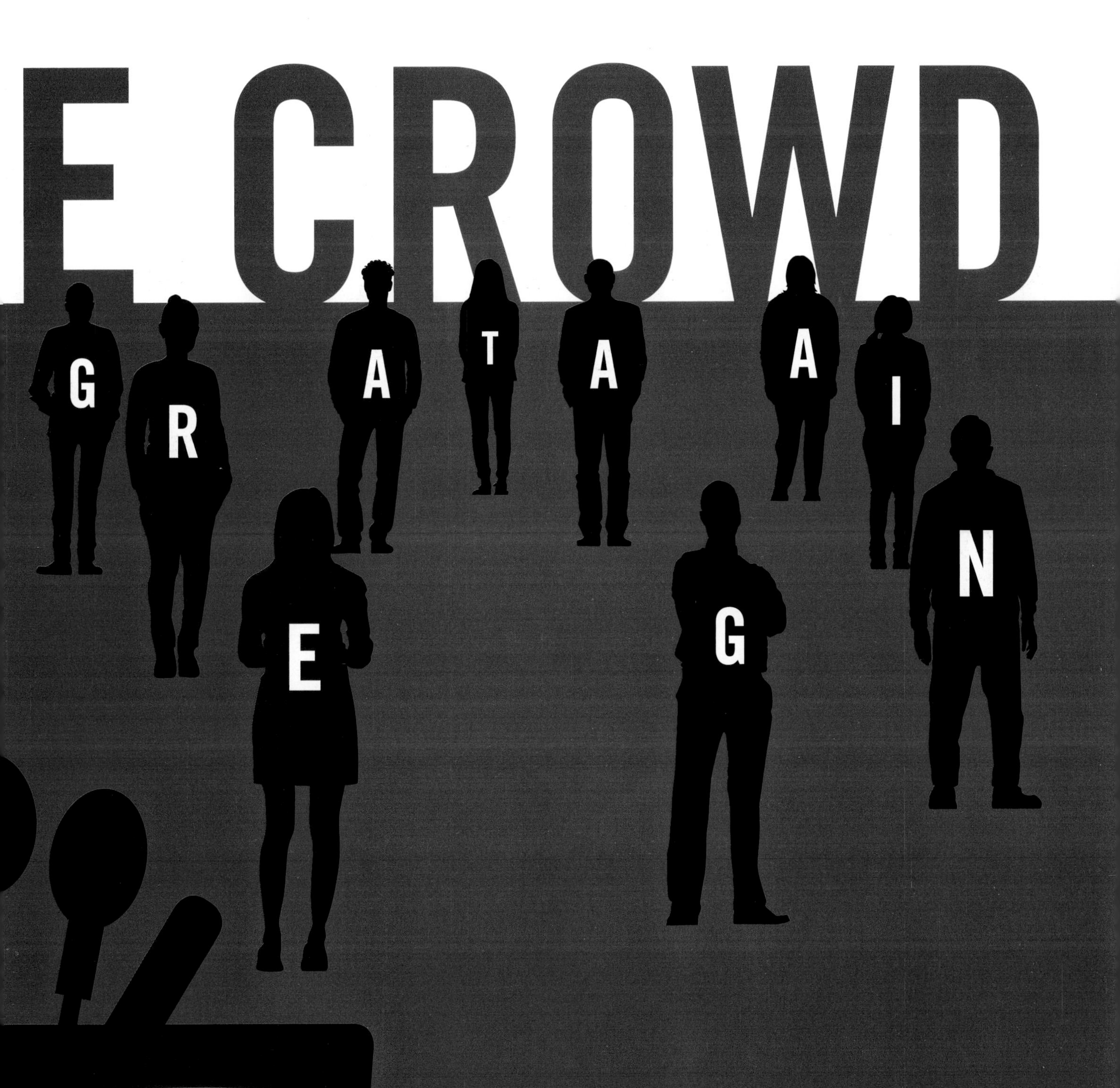

see pages 94–95 for answers

When it comes to choosing a political party, The Donald likes to change horses. Here's how his path to the White House has gone...

POLITICAL PA

1987

(Republican)

1999

(Independence Party of New York)

2001

(Democrat)

RTY FLIP FLOP
2009
(Republican)
2011
(Independent)
2012
(Republican)

Emoji catchphrases

Can you guess the following Trumpian catchphrases from the emojis?

See pages 94–95 for answers

CELEBRITY FEUDS

Robert De Niro

RDN: 'He talks how he'd like to punch people in the face? Well, I'd like to punch him in the face.'

DT: 'Well he's not the brightest bulb on the planet. I like his acting but in terms of when I watch him doing interviews and various other things, we're not dealing with Albert Einstein.'

Bette Midler

BM: '60 Shades of Stupidity: Ten extra points for the terrible dye job someone talked him into.'

DT: 'I never liked @BetteMidler's persona or singing and haven't heard her name in years.'

Michael Moore

DT: 'While not at all presidential I must point out that the Sloppy Michael Moore Show on Broadway was a TOTAL BOMB and was forced to close. Sad!'

MM: 'You must have my smash hit of a Broadway show confused with your presidency – which IS a total bomb and WILL indeed close early. NOT SAD.'

Russell Brand

DT: @katyperry must have been drunk when she married Russell brand @rustyrockets

RB: @realDonaldTrump are you drunk when you write these tweets? Or does that foam you spray on your bald head make you high?

Jon Stewart

JS: 'Did you know Donald Trump's birth name is Fkface Von Clownstick?...'**

DT: 'Amazing how the haters & losers keep tweeting the name Fkface Von Clownstick like they are so original and no one else is doing it.'**

THE DONALD GUIDE TO HANDSHAKES

1. The Elderly Couple Clasp

2. The Marathon (lasting 19 seconds)

3. The Heads, Shoulders, Knees and Toes

4. The stay as far away from each other as possible

5. The Forearm Fondle

6. The handshake–air kiss

What shade is the Donald today?

RACE RELATIONS

'I am the least racist person that you have ever met.' September 2016

'I have a great relationship with the blacks.' April 2011

'Oh, look at my African-American over there. Look at him.' June 2016

'I think sometimes a black may think they don't have an advantage or this and that. I've said on one occasion, even about myself, if I were starting off today, I would love to be a well-educated black because I really believe they do have an actual advantage.' September 1989

'We have some bad hombres here and we have to get them out.' (on undocumented Mexicans) October 2016

'Miss Housekeeping' (on a Venezuelan Miss Universe) May 1996

They would 'never go back to their huts' in Africa. (on 40,000 Nigerians granted visas in the preceding months) June 2017

THE WHI

PRESS ROOM S

FAKE NEWS
FAKE NEWS
FAKE NEWS
FAKE NEWS
FAKE NEWS
FAKE NEWS
FAKE NEWS
FAKE NEWS
FAKE NEWS
FAKE NEWS
FAKE NEWS
FAKE NEWS
FAKE NEWS
FAKE NEWS
FAKE NEWS
FAKE NEWS
FOX NEWS RADIO
FAKE NEWS
FAKE NEWS
FAKE NEWS
FAKE NEWS
FAKE NEWS
FAKE NEWS
FAKE NEWS
FAKE NEWS

PACKING THE DONALD'S SUITCASE

The Donald is taking a foreign trip and has packed all his essential items. Feel free to add anything you think he might be missing...

IMMIGRATION

'I think if this country gets any kinder or gentler, it's literally going to cease to exist.' March 1990

'I will build a great, great wall on our southern border, and I will have Mexico pay for that wall. Mark my words.' June 2015

'We're rounding 'em up in a very humane way, in a very nice way. And they're going to be happy because they want to be legalized. And, by the way, I know it doesn't sound nice. But not everything is nice.' September 2015

'What I won't do is take in two hundred thousand Syrians who could be ISIS... I have been watching this migration. And I see the people. I mean, they're men. They're mostly men, and they're strong men. These are physically young, strong men. They look like prime-time soldiers... So, you ask two things. Number one, why aren't they fighting for their country? And number two, I don't want these people coming over here.' October 2015

'Donald J. Trump is calling for a total and complete shutdown of Muslims entering the United States until our country's representatives can figure out what the hell is going on.' December 2015

'I mean, you take a look at this, it's one way. They get the jobs, they get the factories, they get the cash, and all we get – we get illegal immigration and we get drugs.' October 2016

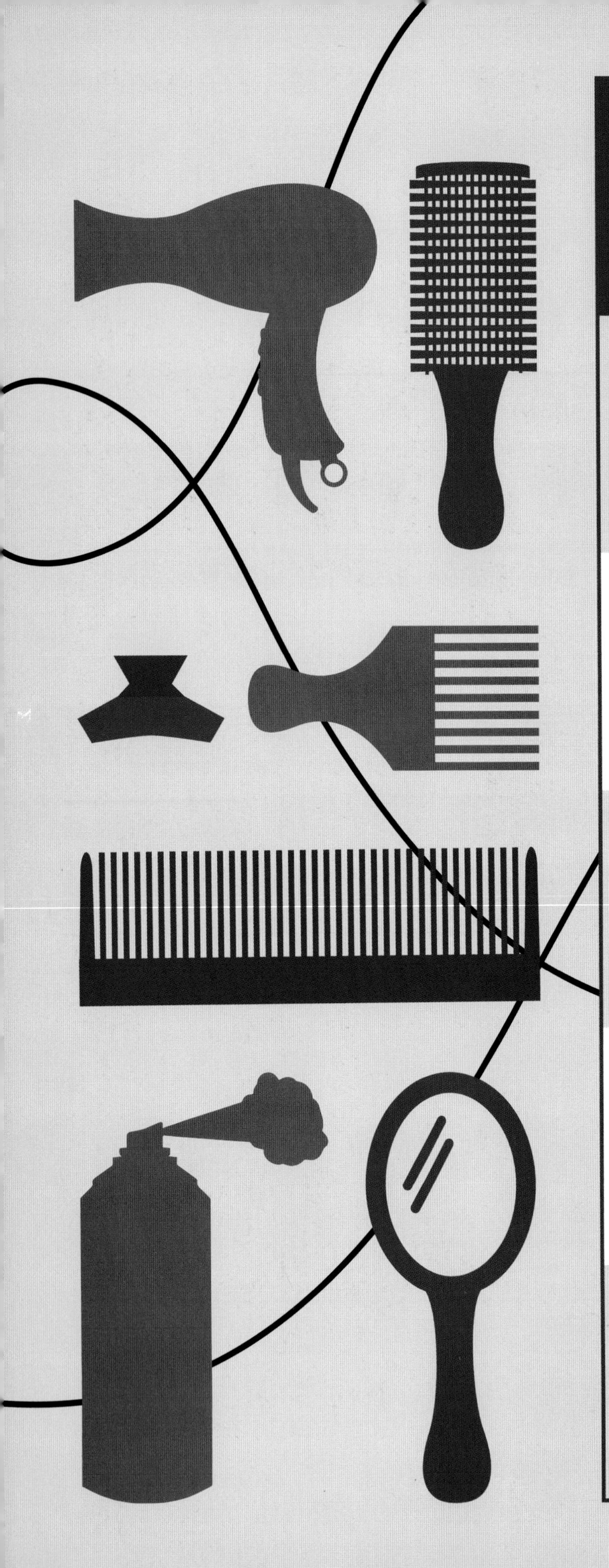

WE SHALL OVERCOMB

1. Blow dry and brush the thinning front portion to the side.

2. Take the longer portion at the back and sweep it forward so it lies at a perpendicular angle to the hair pushed forward in step 1.

3. Take the remaining hair on the top above the left ear and brush backwards to conceal the balding island.

4. Brush the hair at the sides of the head backwards.

5. Secure with a stiffening spray.

Here is a cutting-edge five-stage visual guide to styling the furry Caterpillar around the sides and front of The Donald's head.

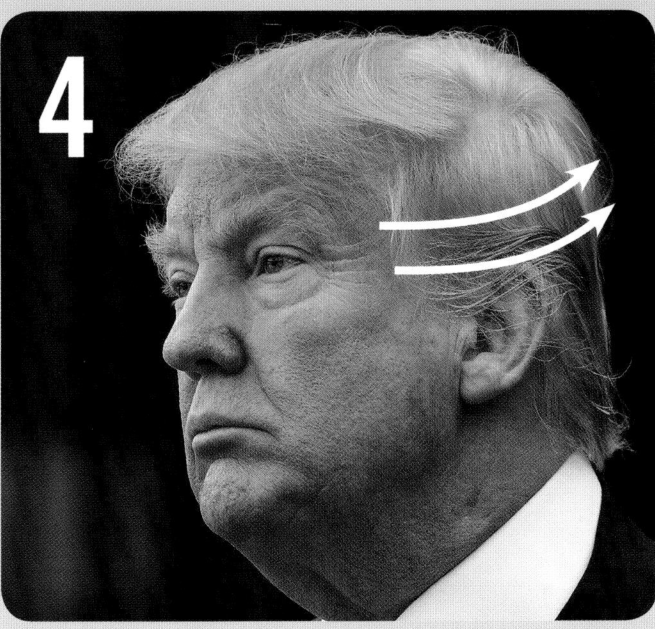

WAR OF T

NUCLEAR BUTTON

DT: 'Military solutions are now fully in place, locked and loaded, should North Korea act unwisely. Hopefully Kim Jong Un will find another path!'

11th August 2017

DT: 'Rocket Man is on a suicide mission for himself and for his regime'

19th September 2017

DT: 'Kim Jong Un of North Korea, who is obviously a madman who doesn't mind starving or killing his people, will be tested like never before!'

22nd September 2017

KJU: 'The mentally deranged behavior of the U.S. president openly expressing on the UN arena the unethical will to "totally destroy" a sovereign state, beyond the boundary of threats of regime change or overturn of social system, makes even those with normal thinking faculty think about discretion and composure.

After taking office Trump has rendered the world restless through threats and blackmail against all countries in the world. He is unfit to hold the prerogative of supreme command of a country, and he is surely a rogue and a gangster fond of playing with fire, rather than a politician.

Now that Trump has denied the existence of and insulted me and my country in front of the eyes of the world and made the most ferocious declaration of a war in history that he would destroy

HE WORDS

[North Korea], we will consider with seriousness exercising of a corresponding, highest level of hardline countermeasure in history. Whatever Trump might have expected, he will face results beyond his expectation… I will surely and definitely tame the mentally deranged US dotard with fire.'

22nd September 2017

DT: 'Just heard Foreign Minister of North Korea speak at U.N. If he echoes thoughts of Little Rocket Man, they won't be around much longer!'

24th September 2017

DT: 'Why would Kim Jong-un insult me by calling me "old," when I would NEVER call him 'short and fat?' Oh well, I try so hard to be his friend – and maybe someday that will happen!'

12th November 2017

DT: 'North Korean Leader Kim Jong Un just stated that the "Nuclear Button is on his desk at all times." Will someone from his depleted and food starved regime please inform him that I too have a Nuclear Button, but it is a much bigger & more powerful one than his, and my Button works!'

3rd January 2018

TRUMP DICTIONARY

TRUMP 1. (noun, c, 1560): A suit that's been given more value than others through birth, rash public decision-making and sheer dumb luck.

2. (noun and intransitive verb, 20th century): To do or provide what is necessary in order to succeed (at any cost to the nation).

3. (noun and verb, c 1550): An expulsion of gas from the anus. Widely regarded as disgusting and repulsive (by approximately 51% of the electorate), but can be rather amusing under the right circumstances.

– 88 –

THE GREAT INVENTOR

The Donald is well known for inventing completely new words and phrases. Here are some examples of his very stable genius in action:

DEVISING THE SLOGAN 'MAKE AMERICA GREAT AGAIN'

The Donald's creation theory: 'I said, "We'll make America great." And I had started off "We Will Make America Great." That was my first idea, but I didn't like it. And then all of a sudden it was going to be "Make America Great." But that didn't work because that was a slight to America because that means it was never great before. And it has been great before. So I said, "Make America Great Again." I said, "That is so good." I wrote it down. I went to my lawyers . . . said, "See if you can have this registered and trademarked."'

Alternative creation theory: used in Ronald Reagan's Presidential election campaign of 1980 and widely printed on posters and badges.

INVENTING THE WORD 'FAKE'

The Donald's creation theory: '...one of the greatest of all terms I've come up with, is "fake". I guess other people have used it perhaps over the years, but I've never noticed it.'

Alternative creation theory: first known use of 'fake' to mean 'counterfeit' or 'sham' was 1775.

THINKING OF THE ECONOMIC THEORY 'PRIMING THE PUMP'

The Donald's creation theory: (To an editor at the *Economist*) 'Have you heard that expression used before? Because I haven't heard it. I mean, I just... I came up with it a couple of days ago and I thought it was good. It's what you have to do.'

Alternative creation theory: already widely used by 1933 to refer to measures enacted to stimulate the economy during a recession.

A Day in the Life of
THE DONALD

5.30am: Wake up. Turn on three televisions and shout 'Fake News!' with joyful abandon.

5.35am: Melania, in her separate bedroom approximately 50 feet away, sighs, and shakes her head before unbolting the three locks on her door.

6.30am: Wash, dry, blow dry, brush, comb, fold, sculpt and glue hair.

7am: Paint face Oompa Loompa orange colour. Wink at self in mirror and whisper 'You're Hired'.

7.30am: Find out what Rocket Man's up to in Korea. Attack enemies on Twitter.

9am: Walk down to the Oval Office to continue doodle of the Wall. Call lawyer to see about copyrighting the phrase 'Great Wall'.

11.30am: Diet Coke break. Think of the exact opposite of the Diet Coke advert.

12pm: Important Presidenty meeting at Trump National Golf Club in Northern Virginia. Remember to pack white hat and cloak just in case.

6.30pm: Retire to bedroom where three cheeseburgers will be waiting. Yell at domestic staff for picking up dirty clothes from the floor. Lock door.

11pm: Goodnight call to Vladimir.

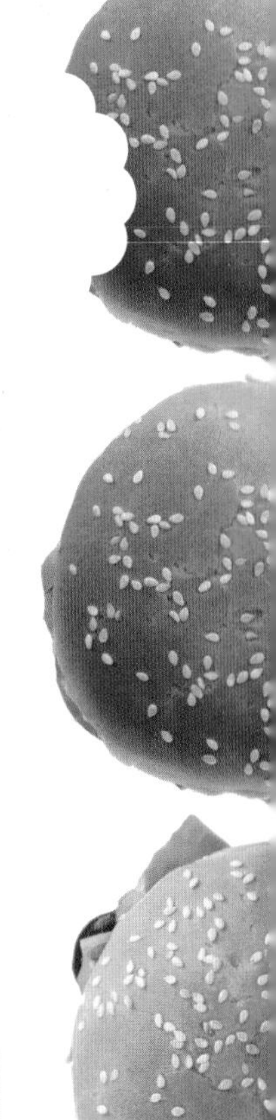

LGBTQ

'First of all, I live in New York. I know many, many gay people. Tremendous people. And to be honest with you, as far as civil unions are concerned, I haven't totally formed my opinion. But there can be no discrimination against gays.' April 2011

'It's like in golf... A lot of people – I don't want this to sound trivial – but a lot of people are switching to these really long putters, very unattractive... it's weird. You see these great players with these really long putters, because they can't sink three-footers anymore. And, I hate it. I am a traditionalist. I have so many fabulous friends who happen to be gay, but I am a traditionalist.' May 2011

'I think I'm evolving, and I think I'm a very fair person, but I have been for traditional marriage. I am for traditional marriage, I am for a marriage between a man and a woman.' November 2013

'North Carolina did something that was very strong and they're paying a big price. There's a lot of problems. You leave it the way it is. There have been very few complaints the way it is.' (on North Carolina's decision to pass a bill restricting transgender individuals' access to bathrooms that conform with their gender identity). April 2016

'Thank you to the LGBT community! I will fight for you while Hillary brings in more people that will threaten your freedoms and beliefs.' June 2016

'Ask the gays what they think and what they do in not only Saudi Arabia, but many of these countries, and then you tell me who's your friend: Donald Trump or Hillary Clinton?' June 2016

'After consultation with my Generals and military experts, please be advised that the United States Government will not accept or allow transgender individuals to serve in any capacity in the U.S. Military.' July 2017

Colour in the Seal

We've made a more suitable version of the presidential seal for The Donald and invite you to colour it in!

ENT OF THE UNITED STATES
SE
FALSUS NUNTIAM

ANSWERS

Match the Comment to the Country

Their 'health system is increasingly self-sufficient' (A: Nambia)
'A total mess' (B: Germany)
'Hellhole' (Trick answer: C: Brussels. Whereas Belgium is 'a beautiful city')
'Shithole' (Will accept D: Haiti and any African nations)
'They're rapists' (G: Mexico)
'A corrupt and poorly run country' (E: Iran)

Donald's Film and TV Cameos

1. *Home Alone 2*
2. *Two Weeks Notice*
3. *Sex and the City*
4. *Zoolander*
5. *Spin City*
6. *The Fresh Prince of Bel Air*

Secret Service Code Names

Renegade – Barack Obama
Kittyhawk – Queen Elizabeth II
Mogul – The Donald (no, really!)
Evergreen – Hillary Clinton
Searchlight – Richard Nixon
Unicorn – Prince Charles
Eagle – Bill Clinton (and President Jed Bartlet in *The West Wing*)
Rawhide – Ronald Reagan
Timberwolf – George H. W. Bush
Lace – Jacqueline Kennedy

Who Said It?
'If you win, you need not have to explain. If you lose, you should be there to explain!' **(Adolf Hitler)** 'The problem with me is that I am fifty or one hundred years ahead of my time.' **(Idi Amin)** 'I play to people's fantasies – I call it truthful hyperbole.' **(The Donald)** 'I'm quite modest. I don't want to tell people I'm a leader.' **(Pol Pot)** 'I trust no one, not even myself.' **(Joseph Stalin)** 'Those who do not love me do not deserve to live.' **(Colonel Gaddafi)** 'I'm not a dictator. It's just that I have a grumpy face.' **(Augusto Pinochet)**

Riddle
The Donald's hair makes him 6ft 3, two inches taller than Barack and his 'hair' (*right*)

Match the Insult to the Person
'Always looking to start World War III.' **(Meryl Streep)**
'Had to bring in mommy to take a slap at me.' **(Mitt Romney)**
'There's never been anyone more abusive to women in politics.' **(Bernie Sanders)**
'Hilary flunky who lost big.' **(Ted Cruz)**
'He just wants to sit down and go home to bed!' **(Bill Clinton)**
'So awkward and goofy.' **(Whoopi Goldberg)**
'Now in total freefall.' **(Jeb Bush)**
'Mathematically dead and totally desperate.' **(John McCain)**

A Hard Act to Follow
1. Piers Morgan
2. Gary Player
3. Vince McMahon. Will accept Mr. McMahon

Count the Crowd
13,751 people

Emoji Catchphrases
1. Grab 'em by the pussy
2. Make America Great Again
3. Very Stable Genius
4. No Call–US–Iron (Collusion)

CREDITS

(obviously)